CW00689841

Finding Joy and Hope in Advent and Christmas

Benedict XVI

All booklets are published thanks to the generous support of the members of the Catholic Truth Society

CATHOLIC TRUTH SOCIETY
PUBLISHERS TO THE HOLY SEE

Contents

Advent: Live in the present moment

With this celebration we are entering the liturgical season of Advent. In the biblical Reading we have just heard, taken from the First Letter to the Thessalonians, the Apostle Paul invites us to prepare for "the coming of our Lord Jesus Christ" (5:23), with God's grace keeping ourselves blameless. The exact word Paul uses is "coming", in Latin adventus, from which the term "Advent" derives.

God coming to visit

Let us reflect briefly on the meaning of this word, which can be rendered with "presence", "arrival" or "coming". In the language of the ancient world it was a technical term used to indicate the arrival of an official or the visit of the king or emperor to a province. However, it could also mean the coming of the divinity that emerges from concealment to manifest himself forcefully or that was celebrated as being present in worship.

Christians used the word "advent" to express their relationship with Jesus Christ: Jesus is the King who entered this poor "province" called "earth" to pay everyone a visit; he makes all those who believe in him participate in his Coming, all who believe in his presence in the liturgical assembly. The essential meaning of the word adventus was: God is here, he has not withdrawn from the world, he has not deserted us. Even if we cannot see and touch him as we can tangible realities, he is here and comes to visit us in many ways.

Contemplate the Lord's presence

The meaning of the expression "advent" therefore includes that of visitatio, which simply and specifically means "visit"; in this case it is a question of a visit from God: he enters my life and wishes to speak to me. In our daily lives we all experience having little time for the Lord and also little time for ourselves. We end by being absorbed in "doing". Is it not true that activities often absorb us and that society with its multiple interests monopolizes our attention? Is it not true that we devote a lot of time to entertainment and to various kinds of amusement? At times we get carried away.

Advent, this powerful liturgical season that we are beginning, invites us to pause in silence to understand a presence. It is an invitation to understand that the individual events of the day are hints that God is giving us, signs of the attention he has for each one of us. How often does God give us a glimpse of his love! To keep, as it were, an "interior journal" of this love would be a beautiful and salutary task for our life! Advent invites and stimulates us to contemplate the Lord present. Should not the certainty of his presence help us see the world with different eyes? Should it not help us to consider the whole of our life as a "visit", as a way in which he can come to us and become close to us in every situation?

Expectation and hope

Another fundamental element of Advent is expectation, an expectation which is at the same time hope. Advent impels us to understand the meaning of time and of history as a kairós, as a favourable opportunity for our salvation. Jesus illustrated this mysterious reality in many parables: in the story of the servants sent to await the return of their master; in the parable of the virgins who await the bridegroom; and in those of the sower and of the harvest. In their lives human beings are constantly waiting: when they are children they want to grow up, as adults they are striving for fulfilment and success and, as they advance in age, they look forward to the rest they deserve. However, the time comes when they find they have hoped too little if, over and above their profession or social position, there is nothing left to hope for. Hope marks humanity's journey but for Christians it is enlivened by a certainty: the Lord is present in the passage of our lives, he accompanies us and will one day also dry our tears. One day, not far off, everything will find its fulfilment in the Kingdom of God, a Kingdom of justice and peace.

The true meaning of waiting

However there are many different ways of waiting. If time is not filled by a present endowed with meaning expectation risks becoming unbearable; if one expects something but at a given moment there is nothing, in other words if the present remains empty, every instant that passes appears extremely long and waiting becomes too heavy a burden because the future remains completely uncertain. On the other hand, when time is endowed with meaning and at every instant we perceive something specific and worthwhile, it is then that the joy of expectation makes the present more precious. Dear brothers and sisters, let us experience intensely the present in which we already receive the gifts of the Lord, let us live it focused on the future, a future charged with hope. In this manner Christian Advent becomes an opportunity to reawaken within ourselves the true meaning of waiting, returning to the heart of our faith which is the mystery of Christ, the Messiah who was expected for long centuries and was born in poverty, in Bethlehem. In coming among us, he brought us and continues to offer us the gift of his love and his salvation. Present among us, he speaks to us in many ways: in Sacred Scripture, in the liturgical year, in the saints, in the events of daily life, in the whole of the creation whose aspect changes according to whether Christ is behind it or whether he is obscured by the fog of an uncertain origin and an uncertain future. We in turn may speak to him, presenting to him the suffering that afflicts us, our impatience, the questions that well up in our hearts. We may be sure that he always listens to us! And if Jesus is present, there is no longer any time that lacks meaning or is empty. If he is present, we may continue to hope, even when others can no longer assure us of any support, even when the present becomes trying.

Interiorized joy

Dear friends, Advent is the season of the presence and expectation of the eternal. For this very reason, it is in a particular way a period of joy, an interiorized joy that no suffering can diminish. It is joy in the fact that God made himself a Child. This joy, invisibly present within us, encourages us to journey on with confidence. A model and support of this deep joy is the Virgin Mary, through whom we were given the Infant Jesus. May she, a faithful disciple of her Son, obtain for us the grace of living this liturgical season alert and hardworking, while we wait. Amen!

First Sunday: Christ brings hope

This Sunday, by the grace of God, a new Liturgical Year opens, of course, with Advent, a Season of preparation for the birth of the Lord. The Second Vatican Council, in the Constitution on the Liturgy, affirms that the Church "in the course of the year... unfolds the whole mystery of Christ from the Incarnation and Nativity to the Ascension, to Pentecost and the expectation of the blessed hope of the Coming of the Lord".

In this way, "recalling the mysteries of the redemption, she opens up to the faithful the riches of her Lord's powers and merits, so that these are in some way made present for all time; the faithful lay hold of them and are filled with saving grace" (*Sacrosanctum Concilium*, n. 102). The Council insists on the fact that the centre of the Liturgy is Christ, around whom the Blessed Virgin Mary, closest to him, and then the martyrs and the other saints who "sing God's perfect praise in Heaven and intercede for us" (*ibid.*, n. 104) revolve like the planets around the sun.

A trustworthy hope

This is the reality of the Liturgical Year seen, so to speak, "from God's perspective". And from the perspective, let us say, of humankind, of history and of society what importance can it have? The answer is suggested to us precisely by the journey through Advent on which we are setting out today. The contemporary world above all needs hope; the developing peoples need it, but so do those that are economically advanced. We are becoming increasingly aware that we are all on one boat and together must save each other. Seeing so much false security collapse, we realize that what we need most is a trustworthy hope. This is found in Christ alone. As the Letter to the Hebrews says, he "is the same yesterday and today and forever (*Heb* 13: 8).

The Lord Jesus came in the past, comes in the present and will come in the future. He embraces all the dimensions of time, because he died and rose; he is "the Living One". While he shares our human precariousness, he remains forever and offers us the stability of God himself. He is "flesh" like us and "rock" like God. Whoever yearns for freedom, justice, and peace may rise again and raise his head, for in Christ liberation is drawing near (cf. *Lk* 21:28) as we read in today's Gospel. We can therefore say that Jesus Christ is not only relevant to Christians, or only to believers, but to all men and women, for Christ, who is the centre of faith, is also the foundation of hope. And every human being is constantly in need of hope.

Second Sunday: May we produce fruit

On this Second Sunday of Advent the Liturgy presents to us the Gospel passage in which St Luke, prepares the scene, so to speak, on which Jesus is about to enter and begin his public ministry (cf. *Lk* 3:1-6). The Evangelist focuses the spotlight on to John the Baptist, who was the Precursor of the Messiah, and with great precision outlines the space-time coordinates of his preaching.

Luke writes "In the fifteenth year of the reign of Tiberius Caesar, Pontius Pilate being governor of Judea, and Herod being tetrarch of Galilee, and his brother Philip tetrarch of the region of Ituraea and Trachonitis, and Lysanias tetrarch of Abilene, in the high-priesthood of Annas and Caiaphas, the word of God came upon John the son of Zechariah in the wilderness" (*Lk* 3:1-2).

Two things attract our attention. The first is the abundance of references to all the political and religious authorities of Palestine in A.D. 27-28. The Evangelist evidently wanted to warn those who read or hear about it that the Gospel is not a legend but the account of a true story, that Jesus of Nazareth is a historical figure who fits into that precise context. The second noteworthy element is that after this ample historical introduction, the subject becomes "the word of God", presented as a power that comes down from Heaven and settles upon John the Baptist.

The life giving Word

Tomorrow will be the liturgical Memorial of St Ambrose, the great Bishop of Milan. I take from him a comment on this Gospel text: "The Son of God", he writes, "before gathering the Church together, acts first of all in his humble servant. Thus St Luke rightly says that the word of God came to John the son of Zechariah in the wilderness, because the Church was not born from people, but from the Word" (*Espos.* on *St Luke's Gospel* 2, 67). Here then is the meaning: the Word of God is the subject that moves history, inspires the prophets, prepares the way for the Lord and convokes the Church. Jesus himself is the divine Word who was made flesh in Mary's virginal womb: in him God was fully revealed, he told us, and gave us his all, offering to us the precious gifts of his truth and mercy. St Ambrose then continues in his commentary: "Thus the Word came down so that the earth, which was previously a desert, might produce its fruit for us" (*ibid.*).

Purification

Dear friends, the most beautiful flower that blossomed from the word of God is the Virgin Mary. She is the first-fruit of the Church, God's garden on this earth. However, while Mary is Immaculate we shall celebrate her as such the day after tomorrow the Church is continually in need of purification, because sin lays snares for all her members. In the Church a conflict is always present between the desert and the garden, between sin that renders the ground arid and grace that waters it so that it may produce abundant fruits of holiness. Therefore let us pray to the Mother of the Lord that she may help us, in this Season of Advent, to "rectify" our lives, letting ourselves be guided by the word of God.

Mary Immaculate: Our light and comfort

On 8 December we celebrate one of the most beautiful Feasts of the Blessed Virgin Mary: the Solemnity of the Immaculate Conception. But what does Mary being "Immaculate" mean? And what does this title tell us?

Defeating the ancient tempter

First of all let us refer to the biblical texts of today's Liturgy, especially the great "fresco" of the third chapter of the Book of Genesis and the account of the Annunciation in the Gospel *according to Luke*. After the original sin, God addresses the serpent, which represents Satan, curses it and adds a promise: "I will put enmity between you and the woman, and between your seed and her seed; he shall bruise your head, and you shall bruise his heel" (*Gn* 3: 15). It is the announcement of revenge: at the dawn of the Creation, Satan seems to have the upper hand, but the son of a woman is to crush his head. Thus, through the descendence of a woman, God himself will triumph. Goodness will triumph. That woman is the Virgin Mary of whom was born Jesus Christ who, with his sacrifice, defeated the ancient tempter once and for all. This is why in so many paintings and statues of the Virgin Immaculate she is portrayed in the act of crushing a serpent with her foot.

14

The good fruit of salvation

Luke the Evangelist, on the other hand, shows the Virgin Mary receiving the Annunciation of the heavenly Messenger (cf. *Lk* 1:26-38). She appears us the humble, authentic daughter of Israel, the true Zion in which God wishes to take up his abode. She is the shoot from which the Messiah, the just and merciful King, is to spring. In the simplicity of the house of Nazareth dwells the pure "remnant" of Israel from which God wants his People to be reborn, like a new tree that will spread its branches throughout the world, offering to all humanity the good fruit of salvation. Unlike Adam and Eve, Mary stays obedient to the Lord's will, with her whole being she speaks her "yes" and makes herself entirely available to the divine plan. She is the new Eve, the true "mother of all the living", namely, those who, because of their faith in Christ, receive eternal life.

The Mother of the Church

Dear friends, what an immense joy to have Mary Immaculate as our Mother! Every time we experience our frailty and the promptings of evil, we may turn to her and our hearts receive light and comfort. Even in the trials of life, in the storms that cause faith and hope to vacillate, let us recall that we are her children and that our existence is deeply rooted in the infinite grace of God.

Although the Church is exposed to the negative influences of the world, she always finds in Mary the star to guide her so that she may follow the route pointed out to her by Christ. Indeed, Mary is the Mother of the Church, as Pope Paul VI and the Second Vatican Council solemnly proclaimed. Therefore, while we thank God for this marvellous sign of his goodness, let us entrust to the Virgin Immaculate each one of us, our families and communities, the entire Church and the whole world. This afternoon I shall do so too, in accordance with tradition, at the foot of the monument dedicated to her in Piazza di Spagna.

Hope in anonymous cities

In the heart of Christian cities, Mary is a sweet and reassuring presence. In her discreet style, she gives everyone peace and hope, both in the happy and sad moments of life. In churches, chapels or on the walls of buildings there is a painting, mosaic or a statue as a reminder of the presence of the Mother, constantly watching over her children. Here too in Piazza di Spagna, Mary is placed high up as though on guard over Rome.

The victory of grace over sin

What does Mary tell the city? Of what does her presence remind us? It reminds us that "where sin increased, grace abounded all the more (*Rm* 5:20), as the Apostle Paul wrote. She is the Immaculate Mother who tells people in our day too: Do not be afraid, Jesus has defeated evil, he has uprooted it, delivering us from its rule.

How great is our need of this good news! Every day, in fact, in the newspapers, on television and on the radio bad news is broadcast, repeated, amplified, so that we become used to the most terrible things and inured to them, and in a certain way poisoned, since the negative effect is never completely eliminated but accumulates day after day. The heart hardens and thoughts grow gloomy. For this reason, the city needs Mary whose presence speaks of God, reminds us of the victory of Grace over sin and leads us to hope, even in the most difficult human situations.

Exploitation in the city

In the city invisible people live or survive who every now and then hit the front page headlines or television news and are exploited to the very last, as long as the news and images are newsworthy. This is a perverse mechanism which unfortunately few are able to resist. The city first hides them and then exposes them to public scrutiny, pitilessly or with false pity. Instead, there is in every person the desire to be accepted as a person and considered a sacred reality, for every human history is a sacred history and demands the utmost respect.

The city, dear brothers and sisters, is all of us! Each one of us contributes with his life to its moral atmosphere, for better or for worse. The border between good and evil runs through every heart and none of us should feel entitled to judge others. Rather, each one must feel duty bound to improve him or herself. The *mass media* always tends to make us feel like "spectators", as if evil concerned only others and certain things could never happen to us. Instead, we are all "actors" and, for better or for worse, our behaviour has an influence on others.

The pollution of the spirit

We often complain of the pollution of the atmosphere that in some parts of the city is unbreathable. It is true. Everyone must do his or her part to make the city a cleaner place. Yet, there is another kind of contamination, less perceptible to the senses, but equally dangerous. It is the pollution of the spirit; it makes us smile less, makes our faces gloomier, less likely to greet each other or look each other in the eye.... The city has many faces but unfortunately collective dynamics can make us lose our in-depth perception of them. We perceive everything superficially. People become bodies and these bodies lose their soul, they become things, faceless objects that can be exchanged and consumed.

Mary Immaculate helps us to rediscover and defend what lies within people, for in her is a perfect transparency of the soul in the body. She is purity in person, in the sense that spirit, soul and body are fully consistent with one another and with God's will. Our Lady teaches us to be open to God's action and to see others as he sees them: starting with the heart. And to look at them with compassion, with love, with infinite tenderness, especially those who are lonely, despised, or exploited. "Where sin increased, grace abounded all the more".

The evangelical law of love

I want to pay homage publicly to all those who in silence, not with words but with deeds, strive to practice this evangelical law of love that propels the world forward. There are so many of them even here in Rome and they rarely hit the headlines. They are men and women of all ages, who have realized that it is not worth condemning, complaining or accusing; that it is better to respond to evil by doing good. This changes things; or rather it changes people, and hence improves society. ....

Faith interprets sufferings and illness

Dear sick people, dear relatives, I have just met you individually, and I have seen in your eyes the faith and strength that sustain you in difficulty. I have come to offer each one of you a concrete witness of closeness and affection. I assure you of my prayers, and I ask you to seek support and comfort in Jesus, so that you may never lose trust and hope. Your illness is a very painful and unique trial, but in the face of the mystery of God who took on our mortal flesh, it acquires meaning and becomes a gift as well as an opportunity for sanctification. When suffering and discomfort are aggravated, remember that Christ is associating you with his Cross because he wants to say, through you, a word of love to those who have lost the way in life and, locked into their own empty selfishness, are living in sin and far from God. In fact, the condition of your health testifies that true life is not here but with God, where each one will find his joy, if he has humbly placed his footsteps behind those of the truest man: Jesus of Nazareth, Teacher and Lord.

A time of encounter, hope and salvation

The Season of Advent in which we are immersed speaks to us of the visit of God and invites us to prepare the way for him. In the light of faith we can interpret in illness and suffering a particular experience of Advent, a visit from God who mysteriously comes to set us free from loneliness and the lack of meaning and to transform suffering into a time of encounter with him, a time of hope and of salvation. The Lord comes, he is here beside us! May this Christian certainty also help us understand "tribulation" as a way in which he can come to meet each one and become for him or her, the "close God" who liberates and saves. Christmas, for which we are preparing, offers us the possibility of contemplating the Holy Child, the true light that comes to this world in order to manifest "the grace of God, that brings salvation to all men" (*Ti* 2:11). To him, with the sentiments of Mary, we all entrust ourselves, our lives and our hopes. Dear brothers and sisters! With these thoughts I invoke upon each one of you the motherly protection of the Mother of Jesus, whom the Christian people in trouble call upon as Salus Infirmorum, and I cordially impart to you a special Apostolic Blessing as a pledge of deep spiritual joy and authentic peace in the Lord.

Third Sunday: The crib of joy

We have now reached the Third Sunday of Advent. Today in the liturgy the Apostle Paul's invitation rings out: "Rejoice in the Lord always; again I will say, Rejoice.... The Lord is at hand!" (*Ph* 4:4-5). While Mother Church accompanies us towards Holy Christmas she helps us rediscover the meaning and taste of Christian joy, so different from that of the world. On this Sunday, according to a beautiful tradition, the children of Rome come to have the Pope bless the Baby Jesus figurines that they will put in their cribs. And in fact, I see here in St Peter's Square a great number of children and young people, together with their parents, teachers and catechists.

Love, humility and poverty

Dear friends, I greet you all with deep affection and thank you for coming. It gives me great joy to know that the custom of creating a crib scene has been preserved in your families. Yet it is not enough to repeat a traditional gesture, however important it may be. It is necessary to seek to live in the reality of daily life that the crib represents, namely, the love of Christ, his humility, his poverty. This is what St Francis did at Greccio: he recreated a live presentation of the nativity scene in order to contemplate and worship it, but above all to be better able to put into practice the message of the Son of God who for love of us emptied himself completely and made himself a tiny child.

The secret of true joy

The blessing of the "Bambinelli" [Baby Jesus figurines] as they are called in Rome, reminds us that the crib is a school of life where we can learn the secret of true joy. This does not consist in having many things but in feeling loved by the Lord, in giving oneself as a gift for others and in loving one another. Let us look at the crib. Our Lady and St Joseph do not seem to be a very fortunate family; their first child was born in the midst of great hardship; yet they are full of deep joy, because they love each other, they help each other and, especially, they are certain that God, who made himself present in the little Jesus, is at work in their story. And the shepherds? What did they have to rejoice about? That Newborn Infant was not to change their condition of poverty and marginalization. But faith helped them recognize the "babe wrapped in swaddling clothes and lying in a manger" as a "sign" of the fulfilment of God's promises for all human beings, "with whom he is pleased" (*Lk* 2:12, 14).

This, dear friends, is what true joy consists in: it is feeling that our personal and community existence has been visited and filled by a great mystery, the mystery of God's love. In order to rejoice we do not need things alone, but love and truth: we need a close God who warms our hearts and responds to our deepest expectations. This God is manifested in Jesus, born of the Virgin Mary. Therefore that "Bambinello" which we place in a stable or a grotto is the centre of all things, the heart of the world. Let us pray that every person, like the Virgin Mary, may accept as the centre of his or her life the God who made himself a Child, the source of true joy.

Fourth Sunday: In search of true peace

With the Fourth Sunday of Advent, the Lord's Birth is at hand. With the words of the Prophet Micah, the Liturgy invites us to look at Bethlehem, the little town in Judea that witnessed the great event: "But you, Bethlehem Ephrathah, / too small to be among the clans of Judah,/ From you shall come forth for me / one who is to be ruler in Israel; / Whose origin is from of old, / from ancient times" (*Mi* 5:1).

One thousand years before Christ Bethlehem had given birth to the great King David, with whose presentation as an ancestor of the Messiah the Scriptures agree. The Gospel according to Luke tells that Jesus was born in Bethlehem because Joseph, Mary's husband, being "of the house and lineage of David", was obliged to go to that town for the census, and in those very days Mary gave birth to Jesus (cf. *Lk* 2:1-7).

In fact, Micah's prophecy continues precisely by mentioning the mysterious birth: "Therefore the Lord will give them up, until the time / when she who is to give birth has borne, / And the rest of his brethren shall return to the children of Israel" (*Mi* 5:2). Thus there is a divine plan that apprehends and explains the times and places of the coming into the world of the Son of God.

It is a plan of peace, as the Prophet announces further, speaking of the Messiah: "He shall stand firm and shepherd his flock by the strength of the Lord, / in the majestic name of the Lord, his God; / And they shall remain, for now his greatness / shall reach to the ends of the earth; / he shall be peace" (Mic 5: 3).

A prophecy of peace for every person

Precisely this aspect of the prophecy -that of messianic peace- leads us naturally to emphasize that the city of Bethlehem is also a symbol of peace, in the Holy Land and in the world. Unfortunately, in our day, it does not represent an attained and stable peace, but rather a peace sought with effort and hope. Yet God is never resigned to this state of affairs, so that this year too, in Bethlehem and throughout the world, the mystery of Christmas will be renewed in the Church.

A prophecy of peace for every person which obliges Christians to immerse themselves in the closures, tragedies, that are often unknown and hidden, and in the conflicts of the context in which they live, with the sentiments of Jesus so that they may become everywhere instruments and messengers of peace, to sow love where there is hatred, pardon where there is injury, joy where there is sadness and truth where there is error, according to the beautiful words of a well-known Franciscan prayer.

Fling open wide the doors

Today, as in the times of Jesus, Christmas is not a fairy-tale for children but God's response to the drama of humanity in search of true peace. "He shall be peace", says the Prophet referring to the Messiah. It is up to us to open, to fling open wide the doors to welcome him. Let us learn from Mary and Joseph: let us place ourselves with faith at the service of God's plan. Even if we do not understand it fully, let us entrust ourselves to his wisdom and goodness. Let us seek first of all the Kingdom of God, and Providence will help us. A Happy Christmas to you all!

Welcome Jesus with a child's heart

With the Christmas Novena which we are celebrating in these days the Church invites us to live intensely and profoundly the preparation for the Saviour's Birth, now at hand. The desire we all carry in our hearts is that in the midst of the frenzied activity of our day the forthcoming Feast of Christmas may give us serene and profound joy to make us tangibly feel the goodness of Our Lord and imbue us with new courage.

Historical origins of Christmas

To understand better the meaning of the Lord's Birth I would like to make a brief allusion to the historical origins of this Solemnity. In fact, at the outset the Liturgical Year of the Church did not develop primarily from Christ's Birth but rather from faith in his Resurrection. Thus Christianity's most ancient Feast is not Christmas but Easter; the Christian faith is founded on Christ's Resurrection, which is at the root of the proclamation of the Gospel and gave birth to the Church. Therefore being Christian means living in a Paschal manner, letting ourselves be involved in the dynamism that originated in Baptism and leads to dying to sin in order to live with God (cf. *Rm* 6: 4).

Hippolytus of Rome, in his commentary on the Book of the Prophet Daniel, written in about AD 204, was the first person to say clearly that Jesus was born on 25 December. Moreover, some exegetes note that the Feast of the Dedication of the Temple of Jerusalem, instituted by Judas Machabee in 164 BC, was celebrated on that day. The coincidence of dates would consequently mean that with Jesus, who appeared as God's Light in the darkness, the consecration of the Temple, the Advent of God to this earth, was truly brought about.

"The Feast of Feasts"

For Christianity the Feast of Christmas acquired its definitive form in the fourth century when it replaced the Roman Feast of the *Sol invictus*, the invincible sun. This highlighted the fact that Christ's Birth was the victory of the true Light over the darkness of evil and sin.

However, the special, intense spiritual atmosphere that surrounds Christmas developed in the Middle Ages, thanks to St Francis of Assisi who was profoundly in love with the man Jesus, God-with-us. The Saint's first *biographer, Thomas of Celano, recounts in his Vita Secunda* that St Francis "Over and above all the other Solemnities, celebrated with ineffable tenderness the Nativity of the Child Jesus, and called 'the Feast of Feasts' the day on which God, having become a tiny child, suckled at a human breast" (cf. *Fonti Francescane*,

n. 199, p. 492). This particular devotion to the mystery of the Incarnation gave rise to the famous celebration of Christmas at Greccio. Francis probably drew the inspiration for this from his pilgrimage to the Holy Land and from the manger at St Mary Major in Rome. What motivated the Poverello of Assisi was the wish to experience as real, living and actual the humble grandeur of the event of the Child Jesus' Birth, and to communicate the joy of it to all.

The nativity scene

In his first biography Thomas of Celano speaks of the night of the nativity scene at Greccio in a lively and moving way, making a crucial contribution to spreading the most beautiful Christmas tradition, that of the crib. Indeed, the night at Greccio restored to Christianity the intensity and beauty of the Feast of Christmas and taught the People of God to perceive its most authentic message, its special warmth, and to love and worship the humanity of Christ. This particular approach to Christmas gave the Christian faith a new dimension. Easter had focused attention on the power of God who triumphs over death, inaugurates new life and teaches us to hope in the world to come. St Francis with his crib highlighted the defenceless love of God, his humanity and his kindness; God manifested himself to humanity in the Incarnation of the Word to teach people a new way of living and loving.

A marvellous vision

Celano relates that on that Christmas night Francis was granted the grace of a marvellous vision. He saw lying in the manger a tiny Child who was awakened by Francis' presence. And Celano adds: "Nor did this vision differ from the events because, through the work of his grace which acted through his holy servant, Francis, the Child Jesus was revived in the hearts of many who had forgotten him and was deeply impressed upon their loving memory" (cf. *Vita Prima*, *op. cit.*, n. 86, p. 307). This setting describes in great detail all that Francis' living faith and love for Christ's humanity imparted to the Christian celebration of Christmas: the discovery that God reveals himself in the tender limbs of the Infant Jesus. Thanks to St Francis, the Christian people were able to perceive that at Christmas God truly became the "Emmanuel", the God-with-us from whom no barrier nor any distance can separate us. Thus, in that Child, God became close to each one of us, so close that we are able to speak intimately to him and engage in a trusting relationship of deep affection with him, just as we do with any newborn baby.

God as a defenceless child

In that Child, in fact, God-Love is manifest: God comes without weapons, without force, because he does not want to conquer, so to speak, from the outside, but rather wants to be freely received by the human being. God

makes himself a defenceless Child to overcome pride,
violence and the human desire to possess. In Jesus God
took on this poor, disarming condition to win us with
love and lead us to our true identity. We must not forget
that the most important title of Jesus Christ is, precisely,
that of "Son", Son of God; the divine dignity is indicated
with a term that extends the reference to the humble
condition of the manger in Bethlehem, although it
corresponds uniquely to his divinity, which is the
divinity of the "Son".

His condition as a Child also points out to us how we
may encounter God and enjoy his presence. It is in the
light of Christmas that we may understand Jesus' words:
"Unless you turn and become like children, you will
never enter the Kingdom of Heaven" (*Mt* 18:3). Those
who have not understood the mystery of Christmas, have
not understood the crucial element of Christian life.
Those who do not welcome Jesus with a child's heart
cannot enter into the Kingdom of Heaven: this is what
Francis wished to remind the Christians of his time and of
all times, until today.

Nativity: Wake up and live in the truth

"A child is born for us, a son is given to us" (*Is* 9:5). What Isaiah prophesied as he gazed into the future from afar, consoling Israel amid its trials and its darkness, is now proclaimed to the shepherds as a present reality by the Angel, from whom a cloud of light streams forth: "To you is born this day in the city of David a Saviour, who is Christ the Lord" (*Lk* 2:11). The Lord is here. From this moment, God is truly "God with us". No longer is he the distant God who can in some way be perceived from afar, in creation and in our own consciousness. He has entered the world. He is close to us. The words of the risen Christ to his followers are addressed also to us: "Lo, I am with you always, to the close of the age" (*Mt* 28:20).

The right way to respond

For you the Saviour is born: through the Gospel and those who proclaim it, God now reminds us of the message that the Angel announced to the shepherds. It is a message that cannot leave us indifferent. If it is true, it changes everything. If it is true, it also affects me. Like the shepherds, then, I too must say: Come on, I want to go to Bethlehem to see the Word that has occurred there. The story of the shepherds is included in the Gospel for a reason. They show us the right way to respond to the message that we too have received. What is it that these first witnesses of God's incarnation have to tell us?

Be awake and fight temptation

The first thing we are told about the shepherds is that they were on the watch – they could hear the message precisely because they were awake. We must be awake, so that we can hear the message. We must become truly vigilant people. What does this mean? The principal difference between someone dreaming and someone awake is that the dreamer is in a world of his own. His "self" is locked into this dream world that is his alone and does not connect him with others. To wake up means to leave that private world of one's own and to enter the common reality, the truth that alone can unite all people. Conflict and lack of reconciliation in the world stem from the fact that we are locked into our own interests and opinions, into our own little private world. Selfishness, both individual and collective, makes us prisoners of our interests and our desires that stand against the truth and separate us from one another. Awake, the Gospel tells us. Step outside, so as to enter the great communal truth, the communion of the one God. To awake, then, means to develop a receptivity for God: for the silent promptings with which he chooses to guide us; for the many indications of his presence. There are people who describe themselves as "religiously tone deaf". The gift of a capacity to perceive God seems as if it is withheld from some. And indeed – our way of thinking and acting, the mentality of today's world, the whole range of our experience is inclined to deaden our receptivity for God, to make us "tone deaf" towards him. And yet in every soul, the desire for God, the capacity to encounter him, is present, whether in a hidden way or overtly. In order to arrive at this vigilance, this awakening to what is essential, we should pray for ourselves and for others, for those who appear "tone deaf" and yet in whom there is a keen desire for God to manifest himself. The great theologian Origen said this: if I had the grace to see as Paul saw, I could even now (during the Liturgy) contemplate a great host of angels (cf. in *Lk* 23:9). And indeed, in the sacred liturgy, we are surrounded by the angels of God and the saints. The Lord himself is present in our midst. Lord, open the eyes of our hearts, so that we may become vigilant and clear-sighted, in this way bringing you close to others as well!

God is the highest priority

Let us return to the Christmas Gospel. It tells us that after listening to the Angel's message, the shepherds said one to another: "'Let us go over to Bethlehem' ... they went at once" (*Lk* 2:15f.). "They made haste" is literally what the Greek text says. What had been announced to them was so important that they had to go immediately. In fact, what had been said to them was utterly out of the ordinary. It changed the world. The Saviour is born. The long-awaited Son of David has come into the world in his own city. What could be more important? No doubt they were partly driven by curiosity, but first and foremost it was their excitement at the wonderful news that had been conveyed to them, of all people, to the little ones, to the seemingly unimportant. They made haste – they went at once. In our daily life, it is not like that. For most people, the things of God are not given priority; they do not impose themselves on us directly. And so the great majority of us tend to postpone them. First we do what seems urgent here and now. In the list of priorities God is often more or less at the end. We can always deal with that later, we tend to think. The Gospel tells us: God is the highest priority. If anything in our life deserves haste without delay, then, it is God's work alone. The Rule of Saint Benedict contains this teaching: "Place nothing at all before the work of God (i.e. the divine office)". For monks, the Liturgy is the first priority. Everything else comes later. In its essence, though, this saying applies to everyone. God is important, by far the most important thing in our lives. The shepherds teach us this priority. From them we should learn not to be crushed by all the pressing matters in our daily lives. From them we should learn the inner freedom to put other tasks in second place

– however important they may be – so as to make our way towards God, to allow him into our lives and into our time. Time given to God and, in his name, to our neighbour is never time lost. It is the time when we are most truly alive, when we live our humanity to the full.

Let us journey towards God

Some commentators point out that the shepherds, the simple souls, were the first to come to Jesus in the manger and to encounter the Redeemer of the world. The wise men from the East, representing those with social standing and fame, arrived much later. The commentators go on to say: this is quite natural. The shepherds lived nearby. They only needed to "come over" (cf. *Lk* 2:15), as we do when we go to visit our neighbours. The wise men, however, lived far away. They had to undertake a long and arduous journey in order to arrive in Bethlehem. And they needed guidance and direction. Today too there are simple and lowly souls who live very close to the Lord. They are, so to speak, his neighbours and they can easily go to see him.

But most of us in the world today live far from Jesus Christ, the incarnate God who came to dwell amongst us. We live our lives by philosophies, amid worldly affairs and occupations that totally absorb us and are a great distance from the manger. In all kinds of ways, God has d us and reach out to us again and again, so that we can manage to escape from the muddle of our thoughts and activities and discover the way that leads to him.

But a path exists for all of us. The Lord provides everyone with tailor-made signals. He calls each one of us, so that we too can say: "Come on, 'let us go over' to Bethlehem – to the God who has come to meet us. Yes indeed, God has set out towards us. Left to ourselves we could not reach him. The path is too much for our strength. But God has come down. He comes towards us. He has travelled the longer part of the journey. Now he invites us: come and see how much I love you. Come and see that I am here. *Transeamus usque Bethlehem*, the Latin Bible says. Let us go there! Let us surpass ourselves! Let us journey towards God in all sorts of ways: along our interior path towards him, but also along very concrete paths – the Liturgy of the Church, the service of our neighbour, in whom Christ awaits us.

Be shaped by God's sign of humility

Let us once again listen directly to the Gospel. The shepherds tell one another the reason why they are setting off: "Let us see this thing that has happened." Literally the Greek text says: "Let us see this Word that has occurred there." Yes indeed, such is the radical newness of this night: the Word can be seen. For it has become flesh. The God of whom no image may be made, because any image would only diminish, or rather d' him – this God has himself become visible in the One who is his true image, as Saint Paul puts it (cf. 2 *Co* 4:4; *Col* 1:15). In the figure of Jesus Christ, in the whole of his life and ministry, in his dying and rising, we can see the Word of God and hence the mystery of the living God himself. This is what God is like. The Angel had said to the shepherds: "This will be a sign for you: you will find a babe wrapped in swaddling clothes and lying in a manger" (*Lk* 2:12; cf. 2:16). God's sign, the sign given to the shepherds and to us, is not an astonishing miracle. God's sign is his humility. God's sign is that he makes himself small; he becomes a child; he lets us touch him and he asks for our love. How we would prefer a different sign, an imposing, irresistible sign of God's power and greatness! But his sign summons us to faith and love, and thus it gives us hope: this is what God is like. He has power, he is Goodness itself. He invites us to become like him. Yes indeed, we become like God if we allow ourselves to be shaped by this sign; if we ourselves learn humility and hence true greatness; if we renounce violence and use only the weapons of truth and love.

A heart of flesh

Origen, taking up one of John the Baptist's sayings, saw the essence of paganism expressed in the symbol of stones: paganism is a lack of feeling, it means a heart of stone that is incapable of loving and perceiving God's love. Origen says of the pagans: "Lacking feeling and reason, they are transformed into stones and wood" (in *Lk* 22:9). Christ, though, wishes to give us a heart of flesh. When we see him, the God who became a child, our hearts are opened. In the Liturgy of the holy night, God comes to us as man, so that we might become truly human. Let us listen once again to Origen: "Indeed, what use would it be to you that Christ once came in the flesh if he did not enter your soul? Let us pray that he may come to us each day, that we may be able to say: I live, yet it is no longer I that live, but Christ lives in me (*Ga* 2:20)" (in *Lk* 22:3).

Yes indeed, that is what we should pray for on this Holy Night. Lord Jesus Christ, born in Bethlehem, come to us! Enter within me, within my soul. Transform me. Renew me. Change me, change us all from stone and wood into living people, in whom your love is made present and the world is transformed. Amen.

St Stephen: The witness of the martyrs

Today, our minds still filled with wonder and bathed in the light that shines from the Grotto of Bethlehem where with Mary, Joseph and the shepherds we adored our Saviour, we are commemorating the Deacon St Stephen, the first Christian martyr. His example helps us to penetrate more deeply into the mystery of Christmas and testifies to the great marvel of the Birth of that Child in whom is expressed the grace of God which brought salvation to all mankind (cf. *Ti* 2: 11).

The civilization of love

The One stirring in the manger is in fact the Son of God made man who asks us to witness courageously to his Gospel as did St Stephen, who, full of the Holy Spirit, did not hesitate to lay down his life for love of his Lord. He, like his Master, died forgiving his persecutors and thus makes us realize that the entry into the world of the Son of God gives rise to a new civilization, the civilization of love that does not yield to evil and violence and pulls down the barriers between men and women, making them brothers and sisters in the great family of God's children.

Christ at the centre of our life

Stephen is also the Church's first deacon. In becoming a servant of the poor for love of Christ, he gradually enters into full harmony with him and follows Christ to the point of making the supreme gift of himself. The witness borne by Stephen, like that of the Christian martyrs, shows our contemporaries, who are often distracted and uncertain, in whom they should place their trust in order to give meaning to their lives. The martyr, in fact, is one who dies knowing with certainty that he is loved by God, who puts nothing before love of Christ, knowing that he has chosen the better part. The martyr is configured fully to the death of Christ, aware of being a fertile seed of life and of opening up paths of peace and hope in the world. Today, in presenting the Deacon St Stephen to us as our model the Church likewise points out to us that welcoming and loving the poor is one of the privileged ways to live the Gospel and to witness credibly to human beings to the Kingdom of God that comes.

The Feast of St Stephen reminds us also of the many believers in various parts of the world who, because of their faith, are subjected to trials and suffering. While we entrust them to his heavenly protection, let us strive to sustain them with prayer and never to fall short of our Christian vocation, always placing at the centre of our life Jesus Christ, whom in these days we contemplate in the simplicity and humility of the manger. Let us invoke for this the intercession of Mary, Mother of the Redeemer and Queen of Martyrs, with the prayer of the *Angelus*.

The human family is an icon of God

Today is Holy Family Sunday. We can still identify ourselves with the shepherds of Bethlehem who hastened to the grotto as soon as they had received the Angel's announcement and found "Mary and Joseph, and the Babe lying in the manger" (*Lk* 2:16). Let us too pause to contemplate this scene and reflect on its meaning. The first witnesses of Christ's birth, the shepherds, found themselves not only before the Infant Jesus but also a small family: mother, father and newborn son. God had chosen to reveal himself by being born into a human family and the human family thus became an icon of God!

God is the Trinity, he is a communion of love; so is the family despite all the differences that exist between the Mystery of God and his human creature, an expression that reflects the unfathomable Mystery of God as Love. In marriage the man and the woman, created in God's image, become "one flesh" (*Gn* 2:24), that is a communion of love that generates new life. The human family, in a certain sense, is an icon of the Trinity because of its interpersonal love and the fruitfulness of this love.

Educational mission

Today's Liturgy presents the famous Gospel episode of the 12-year-old Jesus who stays behind in the Temple in Jerusalem unbeknown to his parents who, surprised and anxious, discover him three days later conversing with the teachers. Jesus answers his Mother who asks for an explanation that he must "be in his Father's house" that is God's house (cf. *Lk* 2: 49). In this episode the boy Jesus appears to us full of zeal for God and for the Temple. Let us ask ourselves: from whom did Jesus learn love for his Father's affairs?

As Son he certainly had an intimate knowledge of his Father, of God, and a profound and permanent relationship with him but, in his own culture he had of course learned prayers and love for the Temple and for the Institutions of Israel from his parents. We may therefore say that Jesus' decision to stay on at the Temple was above all the result of his close relationship with the Father, but it was also a result of the education he had received from Mary and Joseph.

Here we can glimpse the authentic meaning of Christian education: it is the fruit of a collaboration between educators and God that must always be sought. The Christian family is aware that children are a gift and a project of God. Therefore it cannot consider that it possesses them; rather, in serving God's plan through them, the family is called to educate them in the greatest freedom, which is precisely that of saying "yes" to God in order to do his will. The Virgin Mary is the perfect example of this "yes". Let us entrust all families to her, praying in particular for their precious educational mission.

Witness as a family

And I now address in Spanish all those who are taking part in the Feast of the Holy Family in Madrid.

I cordially greet the Pastors and faithful who have gathered in Madrid to celebrate joyfully the Sacred Family of Nazareth. How is it possible not to remember the true meaning of this feast? Having come into the world, into the heart of a family, God shows that this institution is a sure path on which to encounter and come to know him, as well as an ongoing call to work for the unity of all people centred on love. Hence one of the greatest services that we Christians can render our fellow human beings is to offer them our serene and unhesitating witness as a family founded on the marriage of a man and a woman, safeguarding and promoting the family, since it is of supreme importance for the present and future of humanity. Indeed, the family is the best school at which to learn to live out those values which give dignity to the person and greatness to peoples. In the family sorrows and joys are shared, since all feel enveloped in the love that prevails at home, a love that stems from the mere fact of belonging to the same family.

Beautiful mission

I ask God that in your homes you may always breathe this love of total self-giving and faithfulness which Jesus brought to the world with his birth, nurturing and strengthening it with daily prayer, the constant practice of the virtues, reciprocal understanding and mutual respect. I then encourage you so that, trusting in the motherly intercession of Mary Most Holy, Queen of Families, and under the powerful protection of St Joseph, her spouse, you may dedicate yourselves tirelessly to this beautiful mission which the Lord has placed in your hands. In addition you may count on my closeness and affection, and I ask you to convey to your loved ones who are in the greatest need or find themselves in difficulty a very special greeting from the Pope. I warmly bless you all.

His kingdom of love and life

On this Sunday the second after Christmas and the first of the New Year I am glad to renew to all my wishes for every good in the Lord! Problems are not lacking in the Church and in the world, as well as in the daily life of families, but thanks be to God our hope is not based on improbable predictions or financial forecasts, however important these may be. Our hope is in God, not in the sense of a generic religiosity or a fatalism cloaked in faith. We trust in God who revealed completely and definitively in Jesus Christ his desire to be with human beings, to share in our history, to guide us all to his Kingdom of love and life. And this great hope enlivens and at times corrects our human hopes.

Three extraordinarily rich biblical Readings speak to us today of this revelation: chapter 24 of the Book of Ecclesiasticus, the opening hymn of St Paul's Letter to the Ephesians and the Prologue of John's Gospel. These texts affirm that God is not only the Creator of the universe an aspect common to other religions too but that he is the Father who "chose us in him before the foundation of the world.... He destined us in love to be his sons through Jesus Christ" (*Ep* 1:4-5), and that for this reason he even, inconceivably, went so far as to make himself man: "the Word became flesh and dwelled among us" (*Jn* 1:14). The mystery of the Incarnation of the Word of God was prepared in the Old Testament, in particular where divine Wisdom is identified with the Mosaic Law. Wisdom herself says: "The Creator of all things... assigned a place for my tent. And he said: "Make your dwelling in Jacob, and in Israel receive your inheritance'" (*Si* 24:8). In Jesus Christ the Law of God became a living testimony, written in the heart of a man in whom, through the action of the Holy Spirit the fullness of deity resides in bodily form (cf. *Col* 2:9).

A divine plan of love generates and requires freedom

Dear friends, this is the true reason for humanity's hope: history has meaning because it is "inhabited" by the Wisdom of God. And yet the divine plan is not automatically implemented because it is a plan of love, and love generates freedom and requires freedom. The Kingdom of God certainly comes, indeed it is already present in history and thanks to Christ's coming has already conquered the negative power of the Evil One. However, all men and women are responsible for welcoming him into their own lives, day after day. Therefore even the year 2010 will be "good" to the extent that each of us, according to his or her own responsibilities, can work with God's grace. Thus let us turn to the Virgin Mary to learn this spiritual disposition from her. The Son of God did not take flesh from her without her consent. Every time the Lord wants to take a step forward with us toward the "promised land", he first knocks at our hearts. He waits, so to speak, for our "yes", in small decisions as in important ones. May Mary help us always to accept God's will with humility and courage, so that the trials and suffering of life may help to hasten the coming of his Kingdom of justice and peace.

Epiphany: Promise and fulfilment

Today, the Solemnity of the Epiphany, the great light that radiates from the Cave of Bethlehem inundates all of mankind through the Magi from the East. The first Reading, taken from the Book of the Prophet Isaiah; and the passage from the Gospel of Matthew, which we just heard, juxtapose the promise and its fulfilment in that particular tension noted when reading passages from the Old and New Testaments in succession.

Following the humiliations undergone by the people of Israel at the hands of worldly powers, the splendid vision of the Prophet Isaiah appears before us. He sees the moment when the great light of God that seems powerless and incapable of protecting his people will rise to shine on all the earth so that the kings of nations bow before him, coming from the ends of the earth to deposit their most precious treasures at his feet. And the heart of the people will tremble with joy.

Compared to this vision, the one the Evangelist Matthew presents to us appears poor and humble: it seems impossible for us to recognize in it the fulfilment of the Prophet Isaiah's words. In fact, those who arrived in Bethlehem were not the powerful and the kings of the earth, but the Magi, unknown men, perhaps regarded with suspicion, and in any case, not deemed worthy of special attention. The inhabitants of Jerusalem learned of the event but did not think it worth bothering about. Not even in Bethlehem did anyone seem to take any notice of the birth of this Baby, called King of the Jews by the Magi, nor about these men who had come from the East to visit him. Soon after, in fact, when Herod made it clear that he was effectively the one in power forcing the Holy Family to flee to Egypt and offering proof of his cruelty by the massacre of the innocents (cf. *Mt* 2:13-18) the episode of the Magi seemed to have been disregarded and forgotten.

It is therefore understandable that the hearts and souls of believers throughout the centuries have been attracted more by the vision of the Prophet than by the sober narration of the evangelist, as the Nativity scenes also show where there are camels, dromedaries and powerful kings of the world kneeling before the Child, laying down their gifts to him in precious caskets. But we must pay more attention to what the two texts communicate to us.

Logic and enlightenment

In fact, what did Isaiah see with his prophetic vision? In one single moment, he glimpsed a reality that was destined to mark all history. But even the event that Matthew narrates is not a brief and negligible episode that closes with the Magi hastening back to their own lands. On the contrary, it is the beginning. Those figures who came from the East were not the last but the first of a great procession of those who, throughout the epochs of history, are able to recognize the message of the Star, who know how to walk on the paths indicated by Sacred Scripture.

Thus they also know how to find the One who seems weak and fragile but instead has the power to grant the greatest and most profound joy to the heart of man. In him, indeed, is made manifest the stupendous reality that God knows us and is close to us, that his greatness and power are not expressed according to the world's logic, but to the logic of a helpless baby whose strength is only that of the love which he entrusts to us. In the journey of history, there are always people who are enlightened by the light of the Star, who find the way and reach him. They all live, each in his or her own way, the experience of the Magi.

The gifts as an act of justice on a new road

They had brought gold, incense and myrrh. These are certainly not gifts that correspond to basic, daily needs. At that moment, the Holy Family was far more in need of something different from incense or myrrh, and not even the gold could have been of immediate use to them. But these gifts have a profound significance: they are an act of justice. In fact, according to the mentality prevailing then in the Orient, they represent the recognition of a person as God and King, that is, an act of submission. They were meant to say that from that moment, the donors belonged to the sovereign and they recognize his authority. The consequence is immediate. The Magi could no longer follow the road they came on, they could no longer return to Herod, they could no longer be allied with that powerful and cruel sovereign. They had always been led along the path of the Child, making them ignore the great and the powerful of the world, and taking them to him who awaits us among the poor, the road of love which alone can transform the world.

Therefore, not only did the Magi set out on their journey, but their deed started something new they traced a new road, and a new light has come down on earth which has never faded. The Prophet's vision is fulfilled: that light could no longer be ignored by the world. People would go towards that Child and would be illumined by that joy that only he can give. The light of Bethlehem continues to shine throughout the world. To those who have welcomed this light, St Augustine said: "Even we, recognizing Christ our King and Priest who died for us, have honoured him as if we had offered him gold, incense and myrrh. But what remains is for us to bear witness to him by taking a different road from that on which we came" (*Sermo* 202. *In Epiphania Domini*, 3,4).

The cause of love which transfigures the world

Thus if we read together the promise of the Prophet Isaiah and its fulfilment in the Gospel of Matthew in the great context of all history, it is evident that what we have been told which we seek to reproduce in our Nativity scenes is neither a dream nor a vain play on sensations and emotions, devoid of vigour and reality, but is the Truth that irradiates in the world, although Herod always seems stronger, and that Infant seems to be found among people of no importance or who are even downtrodden. But in that Baby is expressed the power of God, who brings together all people through the ages, because under his lordship, they may follow the course of love which transfigures the world.

Nevertheless, even if the few in Bethlehem have become many, believers in Jesus Christ always seem to be few. Many have seen the star, but only a few have understood its message. Scripture scholars in the time of Jesus knew the word of God perfectly well. They were able to say without hesitation what could be found in Scripture about the place where the Messiah would be born, but as St Augustine said: "They were like milestones along the road though they could give information to travellers along the way, they remained inert and immobile" (*Sermo* 199. *In Epiphania Domini*, 1,2).

Presumption closes hearts

Therefore, we can ask ourselves: what is the reason why some men see and find, while others do not? What opens the eyes and the heart? What is lacking in those who remain indifferent, in those who point out the road but do not move? We can answer: too much self-assurance, the claim to knowing reality, the presumption of having formulated a definitive judgment on everything closes them and makes their hearts insensitive to the newness of God. They are certain of the idea that they have formed of the world and no longer let themselves be involved in the intimacy of an adventure with a God who wants to meet them. They place their confidence in themselves rather than in him, and they do not think it possible that God could be so great as to make himself small so as to come really close to us.

Authentic humility and courage

Lastly, what they lack is authentic humility, which is able to submit to what is greater, but also authentic courage, which leads to belief in what is truly great even if it is manifested in a helpless Baby. They lack the evangelical capacity to be children at heart, to feel wonder, and to emerge from themselves in order to follow the path indicated by the star, the path of God. God has the power to open our eyes and to save us. Let us therefore ask him to give us a heart that is wise and innocent, that allows us to see the Star of his mercy, to proceed along his way, in order to find him and be flooded with the great light and true joy that he brought to this world. Amen.

Unity of intellect and faith

Today we are celebrating the great feast of the Epiphany, the mystery of the Lord's Manifestation to all the peoples, represented by the Magi who came from the East to worship the King of the Jews (cf. *Mt* 2:1-2). St Matthew, who recounts the event, stresses that they arrived in Jerusalem following a star that they had seen rising and interpreted as a sign of the birth of the King proclaimed by the Prophets, in other words the Messiah. However, having arrived in Jerusalem, the Magi needed the priests and scribes to direct them in order to know exactly where to go, namely, Bethlehem, the city of David (cf. *Mt* 2:5-6; *Mi* 5:1). On their journey, the star and the Sacred Scriptures were the two lights that guided the Magi, who appear to us as models of authentic seekers of the truth.

Open to mystery

They were Wise Men who scrutinized the stars and knew the history of the peoples. They were men of science in the broad sense, who observed the cosmos, considering it almost as a great open book full of divine signs and messages for human beings. Their knowledge, therefore, far from claiming to be self-sufficient, was open to further divine revelations and calls. In fact, they were not ashamed to ask the religious leaders of the Jews for directions. They could have said: "we will do it on our own, we do not need anyone", thereby avoiding, according to our mentality today, all "contamination" between science and the word of God. Instead, the Magi listened to the prophecies and accepted them; and, no sooner had they continued on their way towards Bethlehem than they saw the star again, as if to confirm the perfect harmony between human seeking and the divine Truth, a harmony that filled the hearts of these genuine Wise Men with joy (cf. *Mt* 2:10). The culmination of their quest was the moment when they found themselves before "the Child with Mary his Mother" (*Mt* 2:11). The Gospel says that they "fell down and worshipped him". They might have been disappointed, or even shocked. Instead, as the true Wise Men that they were, they were open to the mystery that had manifested itself in a surprising manner and, with their symbolic gifts, they showed that they recognized Jesus as the King and Son of God. Precisely in that gesture were fulfilled the messianic oracles that proclaimed the homage of nations to the God of Israel.

A new kingship of love

A final detail confirms the unity in the Magi of intelligence and faith: it is the fact that "being warned in a dream not to return to Herod, they departed to their own country by another way" (*Mt* 2:12). It would have been natural to return to Jerusalem, to Herod's Palace and to the Temple to spread the news of their discovery. Instead, the Magi, who had chosen the Child as their Sovereign, kept this hidden, in accordance with Mary's, or rather with God's own style. And thus just as they had appeared they disappeared in silence, content but also transformed by their meeting with the Truth. They had discovered a new Face of God, a new kingship: that of love. May the Virgin Mary, model of true wisdom, help us to be authentic seekers of God's truth, ever capable of living the profound harmony that exists between reason and faith, science and revelation.

Break with selfishness to a new life

On the Feast of the Baptism of the Lord, this year too I
have the joy of administering the sacrament of Baptism to
some new-born babies whose parents are presenting them
to the Church. Welcome, dear mothers and fathers of
these little ones, and you, the godfathers and godmothers,
friends and relatives who have gathered round them. Let
us give thanks to God who today calls these seven girls
and seven boys to become his children in Christ. Let us
surround them with prayers and affection and welcome
them joyfully into the Christian Community which from
this day becomes their family too.

With the Feast of the Baptism of Jesus the cycle of the
Lord's manifestations continues. It began at Christmas
with the Birth in Bethlehem of the Incarnate Word,
contemplated by Mary, Joseph and the shepherds in the
humility of the crib. The Epiphany, when the Messiah,
through the Magi, showed himself to all the peoples,
marked an important milestone.

In expectation of a different world

On this day, on the banks of the Jordan, Jesus reveals
himself to John and to the People of Israel. It is the first
time that he enters the public scene as an adult, after

leaving Nazareth. We find him with John the Baptist to whom multitudes have flocked, in an unusual scene. In the Gospel passage that has just been proclaimed St Luke remarks first of all that the people "were in expectation" (3:15). In this way he emphasizes the expectation of Israel and, in those people who had left their homes and their usual tasks, the profound desire for a different world and new words that seem to find an answer precisely in the Precursor's words, that may be severe and demanding and yet are full of hope.

The baptism John offers is one of repentance, a sign that is an invitation to conversion, to a change of life, because One is coming who will "baptize with the Holy Spirit and with fire" (3:16). Indeed it is impossible to aspire to a new world while remaining immersed in selfishness and habits linked to sin. Jesus too leaves his home and his customary occupations to go to the Jordan. He arrives among the crowd that is listening to the John the Baptist and queues up like everyone else, waiting to be baptized.

As soon as he sees Jesus approaching, John realizes that there is something unique in this Man, that he is the mysterious Other for whom he has been waiting and to whom his whole life is oriented. He understands that before him stands One who is greater than he, the thong of whose sandals he is not even worthy to untie.

The burden of sin

At the Jordan Jesus reveals himself with an extraordinary humility, reminiscent of the poverty and simplicity of the Child laid in the manger, and anticipates the sentiments with which, at the end of his days on earth, he will come to the point of washing the feet of the disciples and suffering the terrible humiliation of the Cross. The Son of God, the One who is without sin, puts himself among sinners, demonstrates God's closeness to the process of the human being's conversion. Jesus takes upon his shoulders the burden of sin of the whole of humanity; he begins his mission by putting himself in our place, in the place of sinners, in the perspective of the Cross.

Love that saves

While absorbed in prayer he emerges from the water after his Baptism, the skies break open. It is the moment awaited by so many prophets: "O that you would rend the heavens and come down!", Isaiah had prayed (64:1). At that moment, St Luke seems to suggest, this prayer is heard. Indeed, "The heaven was opened, and the Holy Spirit descended upon him" (3:21-22); and words were heard that had never been heard before: "You are my beloved Son; with you I am well pleased" (v. 22). In going up out of the water, as St Gregory Nazianzen says, Jesus "sees the heaven opened which Adam had shut against himself and all his posterity" (*Discourse 39 per il Battesimo del Signore*, PG 36). The Father, the Son and the Holy Spirit come down among human people and reveal to us their love that saves. If it is the Angels who bring the shepherds the announcement of the Saviour's birth, and the star that conveys it to the Magi who came from the East, now it is the Father's voice that indicates the presence of his Son in the world to human beings and invites them to look to the Resurrection, to Christ's victory over sin and death.

A seed full of life

The glad tidings of the Gospel are the echo of this voice that comes down from on high. Rightly, then, Paul, as we heard in the Second Reading, writes to Titus: "For the grace of God has appealed for the salvation of all men" (2:11). In fact, the Gospel is a grace for us that gives life joy and meaning, "training us", the Apostle continues, "to renounce irreligion and worldly passions, and to live sober, upright, and godly lives in this world" (v. 12); that is, it leads us to a happier, more beautiful life in greater solidarity, to a life in accordance with God. We may say that the skies are opened for these children today. They will receive as a gift the grace of Baptism and the Holy Spirit will dwell within them as in a temple, transforming their hearts in depth. From this moment the voice of the Father will also call them to be his children in Christ, and, in his family which is the Church, he will give to each one the sublime gift of faith. This gift, which at present they are unable to understand fully, will be sown in their hearts as a seed full of life that is waiting to develop and bear fruit.

Professing faith and renouncing sin

Today they are baptized in the faith of the Church, professed by their parents, their godparents and the Christians present here, who will then take them by the hand in the following of Christ. Already at the outset the rite of Baptism recalls insistently the theme of faith when the Celebrant reminds parents that in requesting Baptism for their children, they assume the commitment to "training them in the practice of the faith". The parents and godparents are reminded more forcefully of this task in the third part of the celebration that begins with the words addressed to them: "on your part, you must make it your constant care to bring them up in the practice of the faith. See that the divine life which God gives them is kept safe from the poison of sin, to grow always stronger in their hearts. If your faith makes you ready to accept this responsibility... profess your faith in Christ Jesus. This is the faith of the Church. This is the faith in which these children are about to be baptized". These words of the Rite suggest that, in a certain way, the profession of faith and the renunciation of sin by the parents, godfathers and godmothers constitute the necessary premises for the Church to confer Baptism upon their children.

Will and witness

Just before the water is poured on the head of the newborn child there is a further call to faith. The Celebrant asks a final question: "Is it your will that your child should be baptized in the faith of the Church which we have all professed with you?". And it us only after the affirmative response that the Sacrament is administered. Also in the explanatory rites the anointing with Chrism, the clothing with the white garment and the lighting of the candle, the gesture of the "ephphetha" faith becomes the central theme. "These children of yours have been enlightened by Christ. They are to walk always as children of the light. May they keep the flame of faith alive in their hearts. When the Lord comes, may they go out to meet him...". May the Lord Jesus, the Celebrant of the rite of the *Ephphetha* continues, "touch your ears to receive his word, and your mouth to proclaim his faith, to the praise and glory of God the Father". Then all this is crowned by the final Blessing that further reminds the parents of their responsibility to be for their children, "the first witnesses to the faith".

The divine light of faith

Dear friends, today is an important day for these children. With Baptism, they become sharers in Christ's death and Resurrection, they begin with him the joyful and exulting adventure of his disciples. The Liturgy presents it as an experience of light. In fact, in giving to each one the candle lit from the Easter candle, the Church says: "Receive the light of Christ!". It is the role of Baptism to illumine those being baptized with the light of Christ, to open their eyes to Christ's splendour and to introduce them to the mystery of God through the divine light of faith. The children who are about to be baptized must walk in this light throughout their lives, helped by the words and example of their parents and their godparents. The latter must strive to nourish with their words and the witness of their lives the torch of the children's faith so that they may be shining example in this world of ours, all too often groping in the darkness of doubt, and bring it the light of the Gospel which is life and hope. Only in this way, will they be able, as adults, to recite with full awareness the formula at the end of the profession of faith present in the rite: "This is our faith. This is the faith of the Church. We are proud to profess it, in Christ Jesus Our Lord".

Faithful disciples and courageous witnesses

In our days too faith is a gift to rediscover, to cultivate and to bear witness to. With this celebration of Baptism the Lord grants each one of us to live the beauty and joy of being Christians so that we may introduce our baptized children into the fullness of adherence to Christ. Let **us** entrust these little ones to the motherly intercession of the Virgin Mary. Let us ask her to obtain that, clad in the white garment, the sign of their new dignity as children of God, they may be throughout their lives faithful disciples of Christ and courageous witnesses of the Gospel. Amen.

Becoming God's children

This morning I administered the Sacrament of Baptism to some new-born babies at Holy Mass celebrated in the Sistine Chapel. This custom is linked to the Feast of the Baptism of the Lord with which the Liturgical Season of Christmas concludes. Baptism suggests very eloquently the global meaning of the Christmas celebrations in which the theme of *becoming God's children*, thanks to the Only-Begotten Son of God taking on our humanity, is a key element. He became man so that we might become children of God. God was *born* so that we might be reborn.

These concepts continually recur in the liturgical texts of Christmas and constitute an exciting motive for reflection and hope. Let us think of what St Paul wrote to the Galatians: "God sent forth his Son, born of woman, born under the law, to redeem those who were under the law, so that we might receive adoption as sons" (*Ga* 4: 4); or again, St John in the Prologue to his Gospel: "To all who received him,... he gave power to become children of God" (*Jn* 1:12).

Our "second birth"

This wonderful mystery which is our "second birth" the birth of a human being from "on high", from God (cf. *Jn*

3:1-8) is brought about by and recapitulated in the
sacramental sign of Baptism.

"Become what you are"

With this sacrament the person truly becomes a son, a son
[or daughter] of God. From that moment the purpose of
his existence consists in freely and consciously achieving
what was and is the human being's destination. "Become
what you are", is the fundamental educational principle of
the human being redeemed by grace. This principle has
many analogies with human growth in which the parents'
relationship with their children passes through separation
and crises, from total dependence to their awareness of
being children, grateful for the gift of life received and
maturity and the ability to give life. Generated from
Baptism to new life, the Christian too begins his journey
of growth in faith that will lead him to invoking God
consciously as "Abba", "Father", to addressing him with
gratitude and to living the joy of being his child.

"Brotherhood"

Baptism also gives rise to a model of society: that of
brothers. Brotherhood cannot be established through an
ideology or even less through the decree of any kind of
constituted power. We recognize each other as brothers
and sisters on the basis of the humble but profound
awareness that we are children of the one Heavenly

Father. As Christians, thanks to the Holy Spirit received in Baptism, our lot is the gift and commitment to live as children of God and as brothers and sisters in order to be the "leaven" of a new humanity, full of solidarity and rich in peace and hope. We are helped in this by the awareness that in addition to a Father in Heaven we also have a mother, the Church, of which the Virgin Mary is a perennial model. Let us entrust to her these newly-baptized infants and their families, and ask for all the joy of being reborn every day, "from on high", from the love of God which makes us his children and each other's brothers and sisters.

Sources

This booklet draws together homilies and addresses of Pope Benedict XVI, made during Advent and Christmastide 2009.

Advent: Live in the present moment, CELEBRATION OF FIRST VESPERS OF ADVENT, HOMILY OF HIS HOLINESS BENEDICT XVI, Vatican Basilica, Saturday, 28 November 2009.

First Sunday: Christ brings hope, BENEDICT XVI, ANGELUS, St Peter's Square, First Sunday of Advent, 29 November 2009.

Second Sunday: May we produce fruit, BENEDICT XVI, ANGELUS, St Peter's Square, Second Sunday of Advent, 6 December 2009.

Mary Immaculate: Our light and comfort, SOLEMNITY OF THE IMMACULATE CONCEPTION OF THE BLESSED VIRGIN MARY , BENEDICT XVI, ANGELUS, St Peter's Square, Tuesday, 8 December 2009.

Hope in anonymous cities, HOMAGE TO THE IMMACULATE AT THE SPANISH STEPS, ADDRESS OF HIS HOLINESS BENEDICT XVI, Solemnity of the Immaculate Conception of the Blessed Virgin Mary, Tuesday, 8 December 2009.

Faith interprets sufferings and illness, VISIT TO HOSPICE SACRO CUORE - FONDAZIONE ROMA, ADDRESS OF HIS HOLINESS BENEDICT XVI, Sunday, 13 December 2009.

Third Sunday: The crib of joy, BENEDICT XVI, ANGELUS, St Peter's Square, Third Sunday of Advent, 13 December 2009.

Fourth Sunday: In search of true peace, BENEDICT XVI, ANGELUS, St Peter's Square, Fourth Sunday of Advent, 20 December 2009.

Welcome Jesus with a child's heart, BENEDICT XVI, GENERAL AUDIENCE, Paul VI Audience Hall, Wednesday, 23 December 2009.

Nativity: Wake up and live in the truth, MIDNIGHT MASS , SOLEMNITY OF THE NATIVITY OF THE LORD, HOMILY OF HIS HOLINESS BENEDICT XVI, Saint Peter's Basilica, Thursday, 24 December 2009.

72

St Stephen: the witness of the martyrs, FEAST OF ST STEPHEN, PROTOMARTYR, BENEDICT XVI, ANGELUS, St Peter's Square, Saturday, 26 December 2009.

The human family is an icon of God, FEAST OF THE HOLY FAMILY, BENEDICT XVI, ANGELUS, St Peter's Square, Sunday, 27 December 2009.

His kingdom of love and life, BENEDICT XVI, ANGELUS, St Peter's Square, Sunday, 3 January 2010.

Epiphany: Promise and fulfilment, EUCHARISTIC CELEBRATION ON THE SOLEMNITY OF THE EPIPHANY OF THE LORD, HOMILY OF HIS HOLINESS BENEDICT XVI, St Peter's Basilica, Wednesday, 6 January 2010.

Unity of intellect and faith, SOLEMNITY OF THE EPIPHANY OF THE LORD, BENEDICT XVI , ANGELUS , St Peter's Square, Wednesday, 6 January 2010.

Break with selfishness to a new life, FEAST OF THE BAPTISM OF THE LORD, MASS AND ADMINISTRATION OF THE SACRAMENT OF BAPTISM, HOMILY OF HIS HOLINESS BENEDICT XVI, Sistine Chapel, Sunday, 10 January 2010.

Becoming God's children, FEAST OF THE BAPTISM OF THE LORD, BENEDICT XVI, ANGELUS, St Peter's Square, Sunday, 10 January 2010.